Rosa Parks

by Lola M. Schaefer

Consulting Editor: Gail Saunders-Smith, Ph.D.
Consultant: Thomas J. Davis, Ph.D., J.D., Professor,
Department of History, College of Law,
Arizona State University

Pebble Books

an imprint of Capstone Press
Mankato, Minnesota

Pebble Books are published by Capstone Press
151 Good Counsel Drive, P.O. Box 669, Mankato, Minnesota 56002
http://www.capstone-press.com

1 2 3 4 5 6 07 06 05 04 03 02

Library of Congress Cataloging-in-Publication Data
Schaefer, Lola M., 1950–
    Rosa Parks / by Lola M. Schaefer.
    p. cm.—(First biographies)
    Includes bibliographical references and index.
    Summary: A brief biography of the Alabama black woman whose refusal to
give up her seat on a bus helped establish the civil rights movement.
    ISBN 0-7368-1176-1
    1. Parks, Rosa, 1913– —Juvenile literature. 2. African Americans—Alabama—
Montgomery—Biography—Juvenile literature. 3. African American women—
Alabama—Montgomery—Biography—Juvenile literature. 4. Civil rights workers—
Alabama—Montgomery—Biography—Juvenile literature. 5. African Americans—
Civil rights—Alabama—Montgomery—History—20th century—Juvenile literature.
6. Segregation in transportation—Alabama—Montgomery—History—20th century—
Juvenile literature. 7. Montgomery (Ala.)—Race relations—Juvenile literature.
[1. Parks, Rosa, 1913– 2. Civil rights workers. 3. African Americans—Civil rights.
4. African Americans—Biography. 5. Women—Biography.] I. Title. II. First
biographies (Mankato, Minn.)
F334.M753 P3865 2002
323'.092—dc21
                      2001004835

Note to Parents and Teachers

The First Biographies series supports national history standards for units on people and culture. This book describes and illustrates the life of Rosa Parks. The photographs support early readers in understanding the text. This book also introduces early readers to subject-specific vocabulary words, which are defined in the Words to Know section. Early readers may need assistance to read some words and to use the Table of Contents, Words to Know, Read More, Internet Sites, and Index/Word List sections of the book.

Table of Contents

Time Line

1913
born

4

Rosa McCauley was born in Alabama in 1913. Rosa and her family are African Americans. Her parents taught her that all people should be treated equally.

Time Line

1913
born

1918
begins
school

Rosa's mother was a teacher. She taught Rosa how to read. Rosa was a good student. But she could go only to schools for African Americans.

a school for African American children

Time Line

1913
born

1918
begins
school

The United States had segregation laws in the early 1900s. Segregation separated people because of their skin color. White people and African American people were kept apart.

Time Line

1913	1918	1932
born	begins school	marries Raymond Parks

Rosa did not like segregation laws. Neither did Raymond Parks. They worked together to end segregation. Rosa married Raymond in 1932.

 a civil rights march

ELCOME! NAACP EMERGENCY CONFERENCE JUNE 3-6 1943 WELCOME NAACP

Time Line

1913
born

1918
begins
school

1932
marries
Raymond Parks

1943
begins work
with NAACP

Rosa and Raymond worked hard for the National Association for the Advancement of Colored People (NAACP). This group worked for equal rights for African Americans.

an NAACP meeting

Time Line

1913
born

1918
begins
school

1932
marries
Raymond Parks

1943
begins work
with NAACI

Laws in some states said African Americans could sit only in the back of a bus. One day in 1955, a bus driver asked Rosa to give her seat to a white man. But Rosa did not move.

◄ a segregated bus

1955
refuses to
give up seat
on bus

Time Line

| 1913 born | 1918 begins school | 1932 marries Raymond Parks | 1943 begins work with NAAC[P] |

Rosa was arrested. She was fined $10. The NAACP asked African Americans to boycott buses. For one year, African Americans did not ride city buses in Rosa's town.

1955
refuses to
give up seat
on bus

Time Line

1913
born

1918
begins
school

1932
marries
Raymond Parks

1943
begins work
with NAAC[I]

Rosa went to court.

In 1956, the U.S. Supreme Court ruled that segregation on public buses was against the law. Rosa won her case.

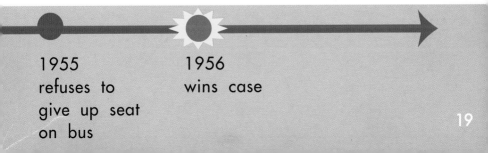

1955
refuses to
give up seat
on bus

1956
wins case

Time Line

1913 born	1918 begins school	1932 marries Raymond Parks	1943 begins work with NAAC

Rosa still works for equal rights. She won the Medal of Honor in 1999. She helps young people become good citizens. People call Rosa Parks the "Mother of the Civil Rights Movement."

1955
refuses to
give up seat
on bus

1956
wins case

1999
wins
Medal of
Honor

Words to Know

arrest—to stop and hold someone who may have broken a law

boycott—to refuse to buy or use a product or service to protest something believed to be wrong or unfair

citizen—a member of a country who has the right to live there

court—a place where judges hear legal cases

fine—to charge someone money for breaking a law

law—a rule made by the government that must be obeyed

National Association for the Advancement of Colored People—a group that works for the equal treatment of African Americans

right—something one can or must do by law

segregation—separating people because of their skin color

U.S. Supreme Court—the most powerful court in the United States

Read More

Holland, Gini. *Rosa Parks.* First Biographies. Austin, Texas: Raintree Steck-Vaughn, 1997.

Klingel, Cynthia Fitterer, and Robert B. Noyed. *Rosa Parks: A Level Two Reader.* Chanhassen, Minn.: Child's World, 2002.

Kudlinski, Kathleen. *Rosa Parks: Young Rebel.* Childhood of Famous Americans. New York: Aladdin Paperbacks, 2001.

Internet Sites

Girl Power: Rosa Parks
http://www.girlpower.gov/girlarea/gpguests/RosaParks.htm

Heroes and Icons: Rosa Parks
http://www.time.com/time/time100/heroes/profile/parks01.html

My Story: Rosa Parks
http://teacher.scholastic.com/rosa

Index/Word List

Word Count: 248
Early-Intervention Level: 22

Editorial Credits

Martha E. H. Rustad, editor: Heather Kindseth, cover designer and illustrator;
 Linda Clavel, illustrator; Kimberly Danger, Mary Englar, and Jo Miller,
 photo researchers

Photo Credits

AP/Wide World Photos/Ron Frehm, 4; Gene Herrick, 18; Richard Sheinwald, 20
Bettmann/CORBIS, cover, 14
Library of Congress, 1, 6, 16; Library of Congress/P&P Division/Materials from the
 NAACP Records, 10 (inset), 12. The publisher wishes to thank the National
 Association for the Advancement of Colored People for the use of these images.
Photri-Microstock, 8; Photri-Microstock/Vincent A. Finnigan, 10